SALINE

SALINE

Kimberly Lyons

Instance Press
Boulder, Colorado
2005

Several of these poems have appeared in *Snare, East Village Poetry, Mirage,* and *The Hat.* Many thanks to the editors. *A Poem for Posada* was first published in a small edition (Situations, 2001). Much appreciation to David Abel and Gary Sullivan for their kind assistance with that project.

I am indebted to the Fund for Poetry for a grant in 2001 and to Olivier Brossard. Many thanks to Omar Berrada, Vincent Broqua, Claire Guillot, and Ladislas Karsenty for their generosity. My teachers, Robert Kelly and Paul Hoover, inspire me. I am particularly glad for Elizabeth Robinson and Beth Anderson's exemplary patience and the inspiration of their creative work. Thank you and love to Mitch and Jackson Highfill.

Cover Image: Brenda Iijima
Cover Design: Anna Moschovakis and Brenda Iijima

ISBN 0-967-9854-3-9
Library of Congress Control Number: 2004116309

Instance Press books are available from
Small Press Distribution, 1341 Seventh Street, Berkeley CA 94710
1-800-869-7553; www.spdbooks.org

CONTENTS

FIRST BOOK

A POEM FOR POSADA

SALINE

*For my mother, Barbara Ann Lyons,
and sister, Daina Elizabeth Lyons*

From a single whole all these things come,
and from them in due time will one return,
that's ever one and many...
often the same will be again, no end
will limit them, ever limited...
for so undying death invests all things,
all dies that's mortal, but the substrate was
and is immortal ever, fashioned thus,
yet with strange images and varied form
will change and vanish from the sight of all.

—Linus, *On the Nature of the World*

FIRST BOOK

THE CYCLONE

There are cracks in my chest.
I wear white on the blind days.
The figs are for Tuesdays.
Soaked sacs, the
dark bags of a ship.
Remember *thunderstorm*
a word
that implicates the future,
sustains across decades.
I carry a burlap purse.
Submerged in dark green
I ride the
cyclone.
My hair
rough as a dog's.
The mind can go anyplace
before sleep, you see.

IT'S A POSSIBILITY

Rough as pencils, the sash flew
myriad polka dots of snow
white densities connect
a choir silvery as a raincoat.
I inserted my paw
in a bucket of the pale, ridged accretions
of a 17th century clock
and ran from there in tartan plaid.
Texas burns in all the air
tires swing in blubbery deposits.

That vault whose
stars pierce
morning
so as to encompass rapture
but not in any way spell it.

I was cold, a traveler
wedded to her sodden coat
on a train who receives clean light
as omniscient as Turkish coffee
or teeny rhinestones.
His breath delivers valentine's raging
ridiculous nets.
The conductor's capabilities
thrifty as lilacs in late April
as evanescent and fluorescent
a pond of purple witchcraft
safely rowing is that possible
the denizens of a poem
coming through the mist whack
a curtain completely uncertain as
to how wavelengths prevail.

CASSIOPEIA'S CHAIR

Linking frayed sky

light burns through broken centuries

electrical appurtenances &
oxidized iron triangles.

I wake up at King's Highway
not myself in a universe speckled pink
of eroded walls & hazy white mausoleums

scribbled across the tongue
the aqua rooms
envelopes in space

manifest location

I'm not "in this"
yet sense its thresholds

like photographing
a mirror
obliterated by a flash

dimension and feeling
stalled in realms.

SOLAR PLEXUS

Like a litany
    an orange dragon
guards against
or solar flares lashing the universe.

Rage against the day
but it's night
the beekeeper harnesses
the intricate jet buttons of its hours.

A stairway
gray hives, the empty eggs
precariously yield
pockets of nothing.

The tangerines of morning
bright definition against
massed interior
now I realize I'm the resistance
I called furniture.
    Plastic infinite waterfall
the matched "Danish" living room "set"
wood squares nervously
pale blue.

I said: *take me there*
but it was an entanglement
of my own dirty hair on my own dirty comb
waiting until Neptune Station
to assemble bright
mismatched portions
while the snow drifts in.

The soul is this ferris wheel
its trapped wonderment

& your red Joseph Cornell
car coat
Polaroid daylight
feb 1967, an aqueous sealed cube
is the body's motions
inhaled vestiges of the century.

The weight in the solar plexus
constellations inhabit
is their sector's inked design

across from a narrow gorge
the lion, the virgin, the carpenter

inflaming solitude with the
inflamed word solitude

as in one recessed cell's
encounter, I wasn't a bird or a
comb
        but was threaded nonetheless.

RED RADIO FLYER

Dial a red telephone and meow
to a cow.

Sweep with a
pink broom
that which accumulates
every hour.

At the moment
which is transient, doubted
and crowded
visualize

a tremulous lavender ball
vulnerably rotating in its
cubicle of the cosmos

bang on a bell, honk on any horn
you have and chug your engine
up a hill
say: *I thought I could, I thought I could*
endlessly row under a falling London Bridge

your punt is coppery, leaf shaped.
Your green truck is now upside down.

Conveyed via
Red Radio Flyer,
a retinue of animals and
cars with transparent wheels
follow you home.
A location inconsistent
as an entirety

you're familiar, mostly,
with corners, spokes

shadows, dust and nickels,
the electrical and miniature.
Home is really a great
blue tent.

Crawl to the edges
ponder
accelerating universe.

APICAL MARISTEM

New trees and sky
the presence between
nothings

a sleeve, a tissue
that falls in the position of
skin

swings from a white cord
mirror in
your lap

consult, come see the snow

a paradox that eventually
breaks down

resemblance

conical light

given a broom, you of course
sweep

the rind of an elephant
labels
of things nobody around here
remembers having had or deleted
just the terms barely remain

a witch in a squashed hat
column of smoke

finds in relation
a rocking horse

with closed eyes

in a million star depths

no one made visible

in the hemisphere's
oblong loop of light

it's the letters that are left

HIVES

Peripheral snaps, like a fly swatter
with no sweat
fits of sound without shape
the kitchen
of September a cellular
lab
ricocheting
from hairs, hives
globs of orange smell
the moon's raincoat &
newspaper dregs
diaphanous in its
costumes the soul
decorated with beads &
bottle caps
words grow inward
edges ephemeral as this page is.

4.31.02

I hate this Sunday consciousness

got hysterical, couldn't find
Lunch Poems, worn thin, wafer of a book.

It's that kind of intensity
generalized, smeared over everything
even this notebook is too
fat & demanding
as oblique, colorless angels
who fill Sunday with old milk
and obligations
look over my shoulder,
like flies.

The spring trees are chartreuse monsters
their fluffy particles
hail down, like ejaculatory debris.

In the dark Mexican restaurant
wrestling and green syrup

the Henrietta Museum

assassinations, witches &
sorcerers

my light, deflected.

2.24.02

The monks in my house
are singing again
and after too much coffee
their linearity of voice
cleanses.

Clouds and light
just before dark an improbable
sense of hills and waves
up near Columbia University today.
Sunday, alone, walking,
bookstores, silence, depression.
My wool gray coat
fluid gray water
flapping.
I love your lover on the radio
(in Trobar).
Water in another form
twists into pellets
and converges

as does the gradual of
Eleanor of Brittany, 14th century
also, *Love's illusion.*

SOAP

I was looking for you
or, more correctly, your
words, in the dark falling on laundry

pulled from stacks: "a new poem" by Wm. Shakespeare
huh? whose orbs of noise clank far off?
My own.

And when I look
everything is inert, like before.

The swollen registers released everything
just before I came through the door

and the return is exact, plus one
increment.

Gradual as a leaf put on
the branch's
casually thunderous
mechanisms, invisibly
hidden in the overall set of elements
I contend with daily, recovery
is possible. In the precincts
of these particular hours.

"Just looking around" I say to myself.
I imagine the words
are looking for me also.
Just for a minute do I think this
like the dirty clothes whose imprintations
can't be smoothed away by soap and water.

Now I read *The Crystal Book*.
Now I accept
how the absence of it yields
to their arrival.

LUNE

After the milk
thins
an emergence of
magnolias framed by grooved green
lips
and a silver spoon fits inside a gray
rim
as the moon, of course, hangs
all day.
Turn out the light
after eating cereal in the middle of the night
in the kitchen
and suddenly the moon
gray as a flower
at the bottom of a bowl of milk.

Space whacks at it
carves out lateral ascensions
winter's first bell
shaped like a Twinkie &
inkling proximity's

slapped by its bluest liminal
scribes, I try and make out
letters in a field.
Red intervals smoldering verticals.
A dark blue bungalow in the Midwest
issues night's manufacture. Its
velvety fabled drapery
a repository of ornate questions.
I can't make out the words anymore.
Condensed, drooling,
elated by instances of knowledge
inscribed and silly,
a participant at last
in the Byzantine structure of the ceremony

dazzled, wake up shouting
the litany's oracular derivatives
a streak of writing the earth advanced

Rum & Coke, Rum & Coke!

SPACE X ACTION
for Chuck Stein

Come so late to any optimism
thin as a red scarf, thin as water
pours off into the lap of prayer
an arena of sparkling non-matter
luxuriantly figurines
surround & compress

a diametric soliloquy

& fancy dolorous lilies.

No minaret could hover
as amply

a cap of nothing

whorls of pinky stars
ignite fissures pulverize echoes

alphabet's sparkling clusters

with my stupid hands

on their slippery boxes

the universe cavorts thus

FAT TUESDAY

Throwing off energy
I only see earth in octagonal wedges
scraped by old papers on a square
crimson plane.
The tremulous uncertainty
of the broken sentence chain.
Knotted chain
be lifted from my neck as morning's silver
line breaks through the night. Irrefutable
awakening & intermittent airs
blow all the crap around winter weeds

throwing off energy.

LIMONATA & NAP

Enamored of sand #56
a sickish pink
the nails of a surfer Barbie

also, of rigid, unripe proportions
of small hot peppers stunk up
with ham and garlic

a giant hole drifts open
in the sky

perforated
a pile of cigarette butts

against a backyard landscape

urgently articulate

the pause, these little spring
puffs

Now I remember sucking on a
REAL LIME

like a secret

at least a hope

continuity

to polar body
the essence.

Reading a book backward
this place was empty
when I used to come here
shadows of Greek postures
everyone wears white
shirts outside my book

  are lavender
words
memory goes between
the segments, a coiled gate
background in the colorlessness
expanded by feeling
inherently without prestige
as a path's odd hexagons
are crooked all the way to
the door.

LIKE THIS

Late August patience
yields strange pleasure
tepid bath on a tepid afternoon
pale olive soap and a sudden
canary yellow leaf
a thunderbolt casually slung from the sky
crosses the path.
Binding my foot, three
shadows
crappy old sandals
have made with dirt and sun
the bravery to wear bright red
lipstick all day.

The sound of generators &
a bar's rectangular hectic night
like this, life has always gone on

all the bright hard debris.
He said: these pinecones
are corns, takes them from the toy truck.
Rigid layers
of my heart
wait to unfurl.

SHIRT

In the white square on my lap
of the foil wrapped edge
around the rusted coils
who waits at an abandoned station
above the circular pool
ringed by their voices
sting the shards at the juncture of trenches
mirrors the resuscitated vines underneath
decorated air's absent vaults.
Blown into black
its site seems green, like a cage
and it's later the chest
bares its gold, a grid of light
our arrival disperses.

Coffee and milk, the hand's undulating flight
a.m. late summer light
presides, withdraws, shifts
lets the harvest down.
Each orange marker
a ping-pong of doubt
and surcease in the wake of all
pendulums.
Anticipated trawls
the overturned alphabets
oblong, stationary, held in reserve.
You could say: *preserves*
and *all of this interval*
by the station silence increased.

TRAIN

Those big bumpy trees
dressed in flaps or flags
today's spiky August light
proceeds
as an archaic tugboat

sometimes, like this morning,
the denotative ejects backward
into my city of white

and behind the skull
the Grand Tetons
bald as pancakes
soberly stir the air
into a different passage
its narrow dimensions
bumpy ghosts
crouched in the dripping underpass

stay put there

Convoluted red tulips
hang down like lamps
and letters jump around the black void
of the sentence
as though sense were only one possibility
in this world
        a contrivance actually.
The intersecting typographies
issue into a space of expandable pages,
a violet empyrean's contraption of radiant circles.

The inside of a cup
is white
and coffee
obliterates its absence.
Now, the space is filled with words. Kawabata. go cart,
Minutia.
Graphic. A pond.

When twilight retreats
then someone knocks on the door.
And night becomes a billowing skin.
Smells intravenously, like hotel soap
or Arabic vanilla
in the dark
on the street of cold water.

SOUL OF AN ETRUSCAN
for Lynn Behrendt

> *Soul of an Etruscan*
> *Soul of an Etruscan*
> lines of Rilke that I
> read on the train
> when I went up the Hudson
>
> a line about
> a bird
> poised on the grave
> monument of a dead man
>
> I kept writing
> in my notebook; trying
> to work it in.
>
> A poem about
> the Hudson River's
> ancient path of silver
> the marshes and incidental
> cottages, the ones by the
> water with a swing set
> out front and picnic benches
> and trash
> and the depths
> of trees, their mute guardianship.
>
> The way the air flickers
> with the shifts
> in weight and sound
> the sound of the soul
> of an Etruscan.
> Rilke himself
> walked the river

the erratic paths
and established boulevards
hearing angels
shift as incrementally
as the wind in
heavy green trees
the original master
of presence
and of absence.

Today, I call out
today, we call out to you
in the infinitely
shaped syllables
that have no boundary
permeated by all of space
I think the word
sounds like *why*

an enormous, engulfing
question as small and
transparent
as a baby's fingernail.

I think you would say:
hold the question
as a halo or
opaque gold raiment
like a woman's dress.
I think the woman
is the earth
and the oceans are
her feelings.

Saline reservoirs
and infinite manifestations
of the kind of life
that needs no light
the self-sufficient sea life
recreates itself and adapts
in splendor in the dark
oceanic night.

All we know is the
river that runs from
old ice.

A man died
and it seemed a crack
opened in actuality
and the possible became apparent
the old voices in a choir
ordered and creative as
molecules that the sun
cleans and gathers.
Our singing.

Even under the ceiling
a secret suburban bedroom's waterfall
polar green stream on Luann's wall
odes in air, trophies, and something called
a ghost fish
hovers inside its transparent tube.
Of the pressures, intensities push back
like big rocks seen from a train.
A strange town's fields.
Feel strange myself, ungathered
intentions spread out and options reduced
a generalized Greek drama
rapture's confinements yield
to the station's complications.
Traveling, hold on the center of sameness
yet I can finally smell trees.
Guards of an unarticulated something possibly
architectural

in a tangled tract

the more inconstant human possibility

cinder of the voices cannot wait.

BLUE COAL
for Keith Waldrop

Broken glass mouth

of the factory's skin

match tip distills in the smoky
rustles dead square rooms

"I love baseball all the time I love it" the boy sings.

All around the mirror of a vanity table's ornaments

debris of construction and recovery

between this morning and tonight

July and August

3:00 and 4:00

lucid fragments sticky

clusters congregate.

A surge of orange
shoots from trees
as though the future dipped her
hand
in our present passage

mark of the hand's
smudged etch-a-sketch

particles on grey
I read, outside Providence,

    blue coal
like an American drive-in movie screen
delphic pool's eroded traces.

TREASURE ISLAND
for Jackson

An archipelago zebra,
time radiates into thin, magical strips.
All night, Pluto shattered.
Zig zags of ice
break the fuzzy vault
of the radio sphericity
of our signaling thoughts.
The black dog who comes to the door.
Is the strangest olden word.
Like the lamp you saw
deeply in a space refrigerated by the universal nothing.
All phenomena in the *wild West Wind.*

LUMINANCE
for Mitch

Tangled little clot could
be a spider pausing,
could possess a dram of blood
carried like a package to
apertures of other black light

first, world goes ash gray, you say
then reignites and flowers
let us live for then
the green world encases our
fabulous multitudinous froth
and incipient diversifications.
Suburban lawns yield tons of
carcinogens
of air born pesticides

how enveloping and fluid
the long grass goes

(length and variety)

bring back the meadows
a Buddha amidst lily ponds
and an antique key
like a rusted lantern
are little pictures to carry

just as much Johann Andrae's:

dawn is about to break, which
after the departure of the dark
saturnine night dazzles with its light

At the crossroads,
you would expect cross hairs,
jumbled branches and day old roses
pressed against a cemetery fence.
I see "Apollo's Agent" like a joke,
ugly billboards in the rain.
Who doesn't hear Robert Johnson
at this place
near King's Highway.
Old Dutch mercantile
and native tribes.
"Accident's casualties."
"we sell gold and silver."
"Violations removed."
Three graces came
as though binding her to their
protections, not the reverse.
Divine features ground
down by too much fate.
Moonlight, which persists
like scissors.
Their four visages
have completely turned to an inwardness
more than any singular thought.
When I saw their clasped arms
and unreadable futurity,
I felt the crossroads
emanate from
our decisive hesitations.

Crossing the Manhattan Bridge
jagged extremities in every direction,
come upon Lucretious:

and such like bodies ever wandering
from the vast deepe, supplies to natures bring
But there's no center to which all things tend
And thus doth this first Booke abruptly end.

A POEM FOR POSADA

for Elizabeth Robinson

SYLVANIA

Old chartreuse haunts
crisscross
ultra modern
ephemerals. Emerald
energies, liquidate and harden
all this month, black beads
in suspension. Gimcrack
décor, like glints in crystal
the eye of an old velvet bag
the witch of September carries
in her reticule
chaos, mirage,
Manhattan and Queens.

A SEQUENCE FOR JACKSON

1. *The Moon Is a Cookie*

As it slid across the sink
wobbling
a pale ear with strange blue windows
intervals of the sky
Halloween earrings
jets fly through.

2. *Anna's Eye Is Wild*

The place on the roof where
the dinosaurs sleep
is there, taking the rain on the tooth
and the green tomato of the earth
bursts and is dry
its big green eye with spikes
shadows, little orange trucks.

3. *I Want My Monster Back*

Our dancing, bony white guy
he will carry a bucket
of candy and rocks
to where the bat lady arises.

A set of black whip
wings
with which to flicker
through this world.

The cup turned over
kinda empty
today. Blank as
the early morning sky
unreadable, firm.
Granulated. The wall's
deeply empathetic blue
magenta contours,
modulated & antique,
yield crystallization's
a sequence of hallways
imprinted on the night.
A sequin pasted on her cheek.
Checkerboard
aridity of the sun's
ascent.
　　　I'm in awe
of its oncoming
thunder
to be transfixed
inhibits anxiety
and the status of non-presence
shapes a container
I project myself in it
or rather
it around me, like
a negative hula-hoop.
The white grid
of any empty hotel.
Kids compare mica and
feldspar
scratched white flints

of the universe's streaming hair,
her spherical dark. I try to
find another word for
"explosive" then
the reversal of momentum
has the ragged shape of
real daffodils.
Raw, withered, green, pale
dry, wet, magnified
dissolved
torn, inclusive, singular
a hive in this sense
midnight's remnants
whirl off
petals, dead stars.

DOLORES

Dazzled as a poloroid
a basilica is a giant husk.
Superimposed, skidding clouds
creamy as a milkshake.
An inherent icy
essence in the process
of dissolving.
I remind myself
its transformation
at work. A thesis
of how thunder emits
fluid, earth spatters graves,
ink condenses into language.

Sarcasm streaks the spacious interior
the spurious inheritor
of every hand on every gold rail.

But I came to her also.
Whatever it is I feel I could become
less of

salvaged long with the
dried brown eucalyptus leaf
curled like a lip
and pods, cones and torn rose cloth
placed there.

SUTRO BATHS

Erato floats wearily silkily
in her weightless bath
of red
    plays the guitar
like the mighty wind
combs through pines
undresses the air
disappears
    under the ocean
lava speeds rocks
crashing out
of the heart
    later on in the century
a rectangular bed
for water
ruins surface.

MUSEUM MÉCHANIQUE

Although I have never been there
it is presumed that it is rightly anticipated
that the dawn will creak in the sky
the giant taut pulleys open the sun
and tiny perfect stars blink off
when the wind jerkily tears the dark away
the velvet coat of our black room
tastes of trees, fur, silver, and gelatin.
You will come out of your bed lucky as a doll
who has been delivered the city's first bicycle
you have plans to travel
into the mechanical mysteries of the skull
preserved in the universe's box
inside the round room of the doll's brain.
And the quartet sings études of the marvelous
for a nickel and a prayer.

PINE REACH

Like a scar on the wrist
a binding
undoes
so that a path
a comb through narrowly parts

reveals
what's ordinarily
hidden as a book
apparent as morning that gradually
evolves
a shape
linear, yet dimensionless.

Robin's egg
crushed into flakes
bamboo stalks the color of a diorama
of bamboo stalks.
Feelings, non-continuous
signals that this odd region
permits. Leaves
the shape of a hand.
White stone marker under fir trees.
Indian and Settlers Cemetery.
Three kids stand inside the the camera's black
frame.
At the ocean's lip, her crescendo and force.
I am terrified
not to dissolve, but to resist.

COUNTERPOLE

I came across the word *counterpole*.
Trees in the Gustave Dore woodcuts.
If words can be guardians or
vertical presences.
As the ninth of the twelfth task.
To originate.
Embroidered pink suns
in which the threads
resembling the rays have loosened.
Construction of some kind,
machines at 4:00 a.m.
The grinding process.
The silence of a figure
entering a forest "at the midpoint
of their life"
Going into the words like that.

MINNESOTA
for Brenda Coultas

The black plastic comb for eyebrows
gummed up by reason is the opposite of what
I wanted to say.
The purple Maybelline eyeshadow resides
in a crumbling pool
incrementally erodes in essence
as if cellular fires whets in becoming.
How the crumbs shelter smaller life forms
inhabited as we are by beings.
A fire wheel, I mean a ferris wheel, twirls
in farm light
and a giant blue man strides in the night.
He wears a dainty red & white gingham
        15 foot shirt.
My first born, a white spider web, a bandage
for the blind. *American Girl* magazine.
The pitch of upper midwestern cool
around August 14th foretells snow and
cessation of all noise in the room suddenly stops
and 3 streams of sound converge, like Harry Smith
said it would.
A cycle of thunderstorms, the word *actually*
also blue perfume, nude hose, the black discs
of 45s wet in the backyard all night long.
Encyclopedia
inside the dumpster.
Gold-rimmed Asia Minor,
history of cotton & Czechoslovakia
I read first.

How did a shazam plastic silver sword
sans sheaf
end up in my crappy purse.
Sword cuts paper? I find it so
relentless
in the spiny vestibules of rain.
The sun has commandeered the earth
its giant head tilts
teased by galactic energies.
The crushed dandelions in September
compressed yellow spikes along the sidewalk.
Glazed with awful light
orangish painted human toes
float then are confirmed
by the word orange
hugely on a black awning.
At the convergence,
the sun's carnival empire.
I've seen your pulsing palaces
mechanized silence under a sweating
pearlized moon
the button of a queen's sweater.
It all burned down.
    Essence of the ocean
via Astroland.

The geometric façade of your skin
of tattoos of white angular deer
at the edge of a cliff.
Hunters wait, sweating
below the ledge in your chest.
I saw in a rectangular mirror
your Norwegian sweater that sailors wore.
The streets slope as though pulled
to some essential cone or pivot.
We walk together among wool piles &
Russian military coats
in the milky absent air.
There may have been used books
and long stemmed carnation flowers. Also,
a Swiss Army knife
interfolded in its metal mouth.
I don't know if labeling this experience
ties it off in some way as
wrapping a wire around a bag of gold
fish in water seals their eventual doom
or constructs a door that allows
us to leave this street
and for others to come through.
In the little black and white film
she repetitively knocked on a trunk.
Objects & manuscripts had been put there.
Was she calling out "Alice"
as though underground?
Filling in the interstices
with narrow velvet strips as a schizophrenic
process or as a bed for the
animals who fall from the ledge?

Jasper Johns seemed to be there
and a small multicolored toy
microscope. The slides contain partial
insect bodies. One half of one wing.
We drank a cocktail of licorice
diffusing in water
out of silver canisters.
In the film,
fish with a brilliant geometric façades
swam among old radios.
What I know of you
and you know of me is inverted.
In the absence, what we
do not know of one another.
What you have made with your hands.
I sense you are building something.
In that place like a market
the interior stuff is brought out
to draw from the light.
A transitional longitudinal zone
a lightening horizon
although the room beams omnidirectionally
as if midnight continues.

A POEM FOR POSADA

On all hallow's eve
they are invisible at the table
drink our orange syrup
drive a bus like a maniac, play a guitar &
adulterate in the mirror.

The dead vote & kick at the moon.

Clothes to wear while dead:
black bow tie, polka dot dress with ruffles
sombrero hat & big old grandmother necklaces or
nothing
which is like clothing in a way
easy to put on and take off
the acts of dressing and undressing merge
until you are pretty much comfortable all the time.

The hills are of a hard black crayon
and the canyons and rivers
thick tracks of white light.

The single light bulb that follows you around
blurts thin jets of lumen
a kind of violet implosion
over your invisible bone head

you get an idea
but you are dead & therefore relieved of its
realization.

The pool hall's glittering green fields
are waiting to be plowed, Señor.

Your arm, Madre,
unfamiliar as a rake on a stranger's lawn,
flickers among the jostling
disappears into the river of their disappearings

the dead are going to a dance at the
ballroom infinity

the music is silvery and spherical
smells of lavender and chalk, of nothing
which is everything, of course, and
elates the nose with its wide open
possibilities.

Grandpere, I remember you as a giant
who made waterfalls out of shells
in the desert of your backyard
now you court Señorita de Maupassant with your
tricky cigarette light
in a continuous day and night
like the films of Buñuel
it remains black and white
in the café of our transparent imagination.
A shack in Mexico seem driving in the rain at night
lit as yellow as a lantern of a grave.

They put white cake at the grave
and crystallized ginger, his favorite food.
The dance a jerky ecstatic dance
wear leis and nutty clamshells
I thought I heard a clacking
when I opened the book and saw the dead
who we are
running around in the towns of this crystal nothing
world.

SALINE

In the ribbons the light makes between night and the window. Objects offer only their parts, only an angle of their face. A cactus seen from a bedroom appears dense as an animal, a hot black being crouched outside on the gravel. The scent of another girl's dresses and her lace church gloves on the white formica dresser strangely suburban in the this adobe house, in this teeming Sonoran desert.

Plastic dolls each drive a flesh colored convertible. They pull each other's glassy long hair, slam their bodies together and have car crashes very five minutes. There is a beige odor associated with their collective. The word corvette or dart or pepto bismol also elicits the memory of that smell.

At night, with a fever, the smell is of my own tongue, swollen and of a washrag. Peppermint pink stripped, it feels alien and particular as though my skin had detached and was being reapplied in rough strokes by a hovering woman. She is shushing but I'm not certain who is making noises or why.

Water pours from a shell fountain improbably situated in the living room. The ticking of a small traveling clock in the brown leather case. These sounds are peripheral and constant. If the sounds are to cut off suddenly then my altered emotions signal that the environment has changed as it does continually, as the sky changes, flooding its big space with corpulent clouds and the renewal of afternoon emptying. The emergence of red streaks of dust.

A streaming façade of visions imply a context, a naturalness to its coded hallucination that dazzles and mystifies. I literally do not understand what people mean when they speak or the motivation of anything that occurs on television. I jump into the waiting arms of my lover, a slim man who offers me a cigarette after we settle into a black carriage. I wear a full dirndl skirt. I smoke a cigarette in the woods.

In this way, objects accumulate. Other people stimulate sequences of feeling with their words and their lack. A person sits as though bereft, arms at his side, looking far across a field, as though looking far inside another person that may be himself. Possessed of words inside therefore filled to the brim with not need of yet another cup of black Yuban coffee.

Like perpendicular shadows, people grab one another suddenly in affection. Rattle drawers throwing everything to the floor while looking for keys or something bought at a drugstore or something found behind papers on a high shelf. A person might scream in pain or seem beset with some feeling while looking for this. People laugh so hard they kick their boots on the floor and tears come to their eyes. People drive around doing errands. What's an errand? It's hard to define, it goes on all winter afternoon. Standing in a store filled with shelves of stereos and amplifiers and transmitters, the snow seems dangerous and compelling, visible only to those who look, as outside is replaced. From a black disc, the swelling tones of Tchaikovsky calls the beautiful and threatening absence. The sound is erased as words are realized.

Shifting granular aggregation flickers as the humans dominate with their frenzied requirements to migrate or fight or stage spectacular rescues. In the night, the children colonize the shadows and branches of the universe's tree. Strewing small dresses, cook stoves and blankets in the grass. The dirt erupts and yields forces which unfathomably have the ability to eradicate and control the human's progress. The sun beams down and boils the hair on your head, yea the very hair on your head.

A haze that smells of cookies and fear and feels like wooden suspenders on your back. Jesus loves the children in their feelings of goodness and badness. I float with Jesus in a large rectangular room of lateral light bars and gilt edges functionless objects. The emptiness of this space is deluxely framed by the edges of knowledge. Jesus carries me in my fear like the brother I do not possess. But at the threshold, I'm put back in my hard chair. He doesn't take us inside there whispering hush and putting his hand to his red red mouth.

In a library in a small town in the upper Midwest, safety and elation floats over the body. The girl sleuths picked their way through a garden of larkspurs. The blue ovals shine like keys to a code in the lavender imaginings of the nursing home's deceptive quiet. Pins forced through the paper as skin is prepped for the cool application of the dream's needle and the lake's envelopment.

The cold wet cement and the hot lake air contain the contradictory satisfactions of pineapple taffy and water. The body made a decision to stay on. As it now craved these curious sensations of life. The mind floats indeterminately above the body and attempts to merge with nonhuman entities for periods of time as a kind of recess. But staying on has its own strange obligations. The passage of utter stillness, boredom and then overwhelming vectors of movement, gesture and culminating excitement. The ceremonies of waiting—as though one is being trained for a war of patience. Like thirsty soldiers in the early days of boot camp, the shapeless suspension of structure both rouses and deflates. There is a coppery metallic reflectivity to the molecules of the self, heavy in atomic weight and dull as a dog's leash.

Feeling in their alien substrate fuse into a shape. Flakes of mica as transparent as skin from the lip.

Does zero equal silence or the noise of everything turned to its highest frequency. Scratching each rock.

Quebec, nuns, a library, an indoor swimming pool. Blue evening. Strange coughing. The funicular's spidery cords. Pilgrim's climb up on their knees up the blackened steps of the cathedral. A tiny shrunken head inside a glass cabinet. The black, long glossy hair, the white nut teeth.

An eyeball in its socket, earth is coated by an a layer of aqueous saline.

Empty of any scent, a blue bottle like a question constant as a shadow. On a foggy November Saturday, burrowing through piles of white rags in a drawer. That which settles around the empty container.

People are realized only partially. Experienced as split forces joined with split forces in my self. From an apartment window, the length of dirty white sill joins to the whitish extended field of snow. These intrusions force a cleavage, splinter elements. Some actions are so drastic and withdrawals so complete that its like a bonfire. The slow accumulation and then sudden disintegration. The blackish pile, hardly differentiated from early winter air, and vestiges of the sun, merge. Body that suddenly houses a smoldering core of feeling.

It's said, trauma produces snapshots of unlinked memory. So does love.

Also from Instance Press

The Habitable World by Beth Anderson

Haunt by Keith Waldrop

True News by Craig Watson